CW00392392

Opposites

Kingfisher

BARTER BOOKS
ALNWICK STATION
NORTHUMBERLAND

on and off

On is the opposite of off.

Sooty has put his hat and coat on.

Sweep has taken his hat and coat off.

Has Sooty got his boots on?

up and down

Up is the opposite of down.

Is Scampi up in the air or down on the ground?

Sweep is sliding down. Whoosh!

Soo is climbing up the steps of the slide.

front and back

Front is the opposite of back.

Soo is standing on the back of the fire engine.

Sweep is sitting in the front of the fire engine.

How many buckets are hanging from the back of the fire engine?

hot and cold

Hot is the opposite of cold.

Scampi is getting a cold drink from the fridge.

Is the weather outside hot or cold?

Sooty has made himself a hot drink.

big and small

Big is the opposite of small.

Sweep is riding on a big horse.

Scampi is riding on a small horse.

Is Sweep's hat too big or too small?

happy and sad

Happy is the opposite of sad.

Sooty is feeling very sad.

Soo is feeling happy.

Do you know why Sooty is so sad?

long and short

Long is the opposite
of short.

Scampi's skis
are short.

Sweep's skis
are long.

Is Scampi's scarf short or long?

fat and thin

Fat is the opposite of thin.

Sooty's bicycle has
fat tyres.

Soo's bicycle
has thin tyres.

Are the trees thin or fat?

fast and slow

Fast is the opposite of slow.

Sooty's go-kart is very fast.

FINISH

Soo's go-kart is very slow.

Is a tortoise fast or slow?

Time for housework

Is the cupboard open or closed?

Is the goldfish fat or thin?

Is the teapot black or white?

Is the hoover on or off?